EXPLORING FOOD CHAINS WITH MATH

Robyn Hardyman

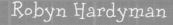
PowerKiDS press

New York

Published in 2017 by
The Rosen Publishing Group, Inc.
29 East 21st Street, New York, NY 10010

Cataloging-in-Publication Data

Names: Hardyman, Robyn.
Title: Exploring Food Chains with Math / Robyn Hardyman.
Description: New York : PowerKids Press, 2017. | Series: Math attack: exploring life science with math | Includes index.
Identifiers: ISBN 9781499431254 (pbk.) | ISBN 9781499431278 (library bound) | ISBN 9781499431261 (6 pack)
Subjects: LCSH:Food chains (Ecology)–Juvenile literature. | Predation (Biology)–Juvenile literature.
Classification: LCC QH541.15.F66 H349 2017 | DDC 577'.16–dc23

Copyright © 2017 by The Rosen Publishing Group

Produced for Rosen by Calcium
Editors for Calcium: Sarah Eason and Jennifer Sanderson
Designers for Calcium: Paul Myerscough and Jennie Child
Picture researcher: Rachel Blount

Picture credits: Cover: Shutterstock: Mark Caunt br, FloridaStock tl; Inside: Dreamstime: Photomyeye 16; Shutterstock: 2009fotofriends 9, AndreAnita 21, Grisha Bruev 8, DonLand 22, Annalisa e Marina Durante 17, Susan Flashman 5, Gerrit_de_Vries 6, Miroslav Hlavko 19, Irin-k 1, Doug James 11, JMx Images 12, Loree Johnson 27, Tory Kallman 24, Lebelmont 15, Martin Mecnarowski 18, Nopparat Nakhamhom 25, Operation Shooting 10, Jonathan Pledger 26, Dave Pusey 13, Scott E Read 20, Mary Sisco 23, John Tunney 7, Victor Tyakht 4, Bildagentur Zoonar GmbH 14.

Manufactured in the United States of America
CPSIA Compliance Information: Batch #BW17PK: For Further Information contact Rosen Publishing, New York, New York at 1-800-237-9932.

CONTENTS

A WEB OF LIFE

Every living thing on Earth is connected to other living things. The plants, bugs, birds, creatures of the sea, and **mammals**, including people, all need each other to survive. This is because all living things need energy, and many get energy by eating other living things. A food chain is a way of showing what eats what in the natural world.

This field mouse is a primary consumer. It eats plants.

Producers, Consumers, and Decomposers

Food chains can be long or short, but every food chain begins with a plant. Plants are called the producers because they make food energy from sunlight. The next link in the chain is the animals that eat the plants. They are called the **primary consumers**. Many food chains then have **secondary consumers**. These are animals that eat the primary consumers. Some secondary consumers are the most powerful animals in the world. When they die, however, other living things, called the **decomposers**, eat their bodies. Decomposers feed on dead remains and break them down. Worms, **fungi**, and **bacteria** are all decomposers. The decomposed remains release **nutrients** into the soil that feed new plants. The cycle begins again.

4

Linking Chains

Most animals eat more than one kind of food. Primary consumers usually eat more than one kind of plant, and secondary consumers eat more than one kind of animal. As a result, they belong to more than one food chain. All the food chains in one place, or **habitat**, overlap each other. Together they form a complex **food web**.

MORE THAN A NUMBER!

CHANGES TO ONE PART OF A FOOD CHAIN AFFECT EVERY PART IN IT. IF ONE SPECIES OF PLANT DIES OUT, THERE IS LESS FOOD FOR THE ANIMALS THAT EAT THAT PLANT. THOSE ANIMALS WON'T DO AS WELL, AND THERE WILL BE FEWER OF THEM FOR BIGGER ANIMALS TO EAT.

wheat

mouse

owl

worm

The owl is a secondary consumer that eats mice.

KEEPING IT SHORT

Animals eat to get energy from their food. They use up the energy by being active, by losing heat through their skin, and in their waste. This means that less energy is available to pass on to the next creature in the food chain. Energy decreases each time it is passed from one living thing to the next. The longer the chain, the less energy there is at the top.

Losing Energy

In a long food chain, a lot of energy is lost on the way to the top. For example, grass makes energy from sunlight. An area of grass can support a large number of grasshoppers that eat it. That number of grasshoppers can feed a smaller number of rats, however. That number of rats can feed an even smaller number of snakes, and finally, that number of snakes can feed an even smaller number of hawks. The hawks are at the top of the food chain. There are far fewer hawks in that area of grass than there are grasshoppers.

This hawk is eating a snake. There are fewer hawks at the top of the chain than there are snakes farther down it.

Short and Sweet

In short food chains, less energy is lost between the bottom and the top. This means that the animal at the top can be bigger because it gets more energy from its food. If they are not bigger, animals at the top of the chain are more numerous because they can breed successfully. This is why baleen whales are so big. Their food chain is very short. They eat thousands of tiny animals called krill. The krill eat thousands of even smaller plants called phytoplankton. They are the beginning of the food chain.

Baleen whales eat krill, which keeps their food chain short.

MATH ATTACK!

The shortest food chain has just two levels, a producer and a consumer. A good example is bamboo and giant pandas. Pandas eat only bamboo, and nothing eats pandas. The chain is short, so little energy is lost and pandas are large. If a panda eats 40 pounds (18 kg) of bamboo every day, how much bamboo will it have eaten in 2 weeks? Use this calculation to help you solve the problem:

7 DAYS X 2 WEEKS = ? DAYS

40 POUNDS X ? DAYS = ? POUNDS OF BAMBOO

Make Your Own Food

Every food chain and food web begins with sunlight. The energy in sunlight is what makes all life on our planet possible. However, that energy must be turned into food energy for us to make use of it. The living things that do this all day, every day, are plants.

Plants capture the energy in sunlight and turn it into food.

Producers

Plants are called the producers of the food chain because they produce, or make, their own food. They do this using sunlight, water from the ground, and a gas in the air called carbon dioxide. Together, they make a sugary substance called glucose, and this is their food. This process is called **photosynthesis**. During photosynthesis, the gas oxygen is created. It is released into the air through plant leaves. This is very good news for animals because they need to breathe in oxygen to live. Plants are the major source of oxygen on Earth.

Sun or Shade

If plants make their food from sunlight, how can some plants live in the shade? If they need water, too, how can they live in very dry places? The answer is that different species of plant need different amounts of sunlight and water. Some need to be in bright sunlight all day. Others prefer it to be shady. Plants **adapt** to suit the habitats where they live. In very dry places, for example, plants have fleshy stems and leaves that can hold onto the water that is available. Wherever plants are growing, there will be animals higher up the food chain wanting to eat them.

Plants can be small, like these flowers on a prairie, or huge like the tallest trees in the rain forest. They are all producers in a food chain.

MORE THAN A NUMBER!

THERE ARE ABOUT 400,000 SPECIES OF FLOWERING PLANTS IN THE WORLD. NEW SPECIES ARE BEING DISCOVERED ALL THE TIME, SO THIS NUMBER IS ALWAYS CHANGING.

PLANT EATERS

leaf

caterpillar

bird

On the second level in a food chain are the consumers. Some consumers eat only plants. They are called herbivores, and they are the primary consumers. Herbivores eat a wide variety of plant diets. Some eat mainly fruit, but others eat mostly grass.

So Much Variety

Herbivores come in all shapes and sizes. Some are insects, such as caterpillars. The caterpillars of monarch butterflies eat the leaves of the milkweed plant. Birds and lizards eat the caterpillars. Other birds can be herbivores. Macaws, for example, live in the rain forests of South America. They eat plant foods, such as seeds, nuts, leaves, berries, and flowers. Their **predators**, the animals that eat them, are snakes and **birds of prey**.

Macaws live in the rain forest, where plants are plentiful.

10

On Top of the Chain

Not all herbivores are eaten by other animals. Some are at the top of short food chains. They are large animals, and although they may not be interested in eating us, they are still dangerous. Adult gorillas in Africa, for example, are herbivores that no other animal preys on. Sometimes, a leopard may attack a baby gorilla, but an adult male gorilla can be very **aggressive**. In the United States, bison are powerful herbivores that eat mainly grass. It would take a whole pack of wolves to bring down one bison.

This bison is at the top of a short food chain.

MATH ATTACK!

The cassowary bird of Australia is a powerful herbivore that eats mostly fruit. It reaches 60 to 80 inches (150 to 200 cm) tall, and up to 120 pounds (54 kg) in weight. It cannot fly but it has a very powerful kick that it uses to attack anything that threatens its chicks. Dagger-like claws on each foot can kill a dog or even a person. If 3 cassowaries, each weighing 105 pounds (48 kg), were weighed, what would be their combined weight? Use this calculation to help you solve the problem:

105 POUNDS X 3 = ? POUNDS

HERBIVORE CHAMPION

The most powerful and deadly herbivore in the world is the hippopotamus. This huge animal may not look very scary, but it kills more people in Africa than lions, leopards, or elephants. Beware the beast that lurks in the water!

King of the Water

The hippo is definitely the king of its food chain. No animal would dare to attack one. Even crocodiles keep well away because a hippo's huge jaws and powerful teeth can kill a crocodile. However, hippos eat only vegetation, in the water and on land. Why, then, are they so aggressive if they do not need to eat other animals? The reason is that they are fierce in defending their young from attack. Even though they are big and bulky, with short legs, hippos are super speedy on land. They can easily run faster than a person, and have been recorded running at 30 miles per hour (48 km/h) over a short distance.

Hippos live in the water by day to keep cool, and move onto land to feed toward night.

A Lot of Grass

Hippos live mostly in the water, to keep cool. They like to stay underwater, but will automatically come up to the surface to breathe every 3 to 5 minutes, even when they are asleep. In the cool of the night, they spend a few hours on land to eat, when they can devour 88 pounds (40 kg) of grass in one meal.

MORE THAN A NUMBER!

HIPPOS ARE SOME OF THE BIGGEST ANIMALS IN AFRICA. THEY CAN WEIGH UP TO 9,900 POUNDS (4,500 KG). THEY ALSO HAVE THE BIGGEST MOUTH OF ANY LAND ANIMAL. IT CAN OPEN UP TO 3.3 FEET (1 M) WIDE. THEIR NAME MEANS "RIVER HORSE" IN ANCIENT GREEK, AND THEY CAN LIVE FOR UP TO 45 YEARS.

A hippo's mouth can open wider than any other land animal's.

MEAT EATERS

Secondary consumers eat the primary consumers, the herbivores. Animals that eat the flesh of other animals are called carnivores. Many carnivores are the champion predators of the natural world.

Specialties

Cats can eat only meat, which makes them excellent hunters. They have powerful legs for catching their **prey**, sharp claws and teeth for killing it, and strong jaws for eating it. Within the large group of meat eaters, there is an amazing variety of diets. Some carnivores specialize in hunting one kind of food. For example, many sea turtles are spongivores: they eat only animals called sea sponges. Some birds of prey, such as hawks and falcons, are avivores. This means they eat mainly other birds. Ovivores mostly eat eggs. Many snakes are ovivores.

Cats cannot digest plants at all. They can eat only meat.

Raptors and Scavengers

Birds of prey and other top bird predators are called raptors. Some of them, such as peregrine falcons, dive at incredible speeds to catch a meal. Hawks sometimes kill the birds they catch by squeezing them to death or holding them underwater. Barn owls swallow their prey whole. Some carnivores feed on animals that are already dead. They are called **scavengers**. Vultures are scavengers. They feed on the bodies of dead animals caught by other hunters, and they often eat in groups.

Vultures are scavengers that feed on animals that are already dead. Their sharp beaks are perfect for tearing meat.

MATH ATTACK!

A peregrine falcon can dive at 240 miles per hour (385 km/h), while a golden eagle, another bird of prey, can dive at 190 miles per hour (305 km/h). How much faster is the peregrine falcon than the golden eagle? Use this calculation to help you solve the problem:

240 MILES PER HOUR – 190 MILES PER HOUR = ? MILES PER HOUR FASTER

CARNIVORE KING

Sharks are fierce predators at the top of many food chains. Sharks hunt fish and other sea animals, which feed on smaller fish or shellfish. Most ocean food chains have plankton at the bottom. Plankton are tiny animals and plants that float on the surface of the ocean. Each animal in the chain is linked to the living things above and below it.

plankton

tuna

marlin

shark

Great white sharks attack their prey by swimming up from the depths and biting with huge force.

In for the Kill!

Sharks are deadly killers that hunt their prey with **stealth** and skill. They can hear, smell, and see extremely well. Sharks can sense prey that is almost a mile away. They can see moving objects even in murky water. Sharks are attracted to low, irregular sounds that hurt or dying prey make.

Blue sharks are ocean roamers. They swim great distances, searching for prey.

MORE THAN A NUMBER!

SHARKS HAVE HUNDREDS OF TEETH, AND WHEN ONE FALLS OUT, ANOTHER GROWS TO REPLACE IT. ALL SHARKS HAVE GILLS, OR SLITS IN THEIR SIDES, FOR BREATHING. THEY ARE NOT SCALY, LIKE FISH. INSTEAD, THEIR SKIN IS COVERED IN TINY THORNS THAT ARE VERY SHARP.

As the shark closes in, it circles its prey or attacks from below. The shark moves so fast it usually takes its prey by surprise. Large sharks often kill their prey instantly. If the unlucky animal struggles, however, the noise of splashing soon attracts other sharks, which join the attack.

OMNIVORES

Omnivores are secondary consumers that eat both plants and other animals. This varied diet allows them to live in many different kinds of habitats around the world. Omnivores can adapt to what is available to eat according to the weather, the season, or the landscape. This helps them survive well and makes them highly successful animals.

This macaque monkey is taking a bird's nest to eat the eggs inside.

A Wide Variety

Animals of all kinds and sizes are omnivores, including people. Most birds are omnivores. They eat worms and snails, for example, as well as seeds and fruits. Ostriches are very large birds, so they need to eat a lot of food. They graze on plants and grasses, but they also eat lizards and insects. You do not have to be big to be an omnivore. Some insects are omnivores, too. Ants, for example, eat seeds and the sugary nectar from flowers, but they also prey on other insects. Many monkeys are omnivores. They eat a lot of fruits and leaves, but they also like to eat insects and eggs.

Eat and Be Eaten

Many omnivores are medium in size, such as pigs, raccoons, and foxes. Raccoons eat insects, frogs, and eggs, as well as fruits and vegetables, and the contents of our garbage cans. They can be eaten by snakes, wolves, and coyotes, though they are good at climbing trees to escape from their predators. Raccoons are skilled at living in many different places. They can live in forests, marshes, prairies, and even in cities. Their long fingers are perfect for finding and eating food. Most omnivores other than humans are eaten by other animals. Monkeys are eaten by snakes, big cats, and crocodiles, for example.

Raccoons will eat almost anything, which is why they can be a pest to humans.

MATH ATTACK!

Raccoons are up to 28 inches (70 cm) long, and weigh about 12 to 16 pounds (5 to 7 kg). Most live for 5 to 6 years, though they can live to be 15 years old. If one raccoon lives to the age of 15, and another lives to the age of 5, how many times longer did the first raccoon live than the second? Use this calculation to help you solve the problem:

15 YEARS ÷ 5 YEARS = ? TIMES LONGER

Omnivore Champion

The grizzly bear is the champion of the omnivores. This bear is most definitely at the top of its food chain, and is therefore called an apex predator. No other animal would dare to attack a fully grown grizzly.

The grizzly bear is the apex predator in the wilds of Alaska and Canada.

Delicious Diet

Grizzlies are brown bears. Grizzled means "sprinkled with gray," and these bears have white and tan tips on their fur. The foods at the start of their food chain are nuts, berries, fruits, leaves, and roots. They eat a huge amount of these because they need a lot of food to keep their large bodies healthy. The next level is the primary consumers. These include fish, rodents, deer, and moose. At the time of year when salmon swim upstream, bears gather in the water to catch them with their long claws. They provide a good source of fat for the winter ahead.

A Long Winter

Although they can be fierce, grizzlies spend 4 to 6 months of each year asleep, or hibernating, in their den. During this time, their heart beats much more slowly, down from about 70 beats per minute to about 10 beats per minute. They live off the fat they made in their bodies when they were active and eating. Still, by the spring, when grizzlies wake up, they have lost about one-third of their weight.

MORE THAN A NUMBER!

A GRIZZLY BEAR CAN RUN AT UP TO 30 MILES PER HOUR (48 KM/H), EVEN THOUGH IT IS BIG AND HEAVY. AN ADULT MALE CAN WEIGH AS MUCH AS 800 POUNDS (360 KG) AND CAN BE 5 TO 8 FEET (1.5 TO 2.5 M) TALL WHEN STANDING.

Grizzlies have power and speed in the water when they catch salmon to eat.

21

Food Chains in the Desert

Every food chain starts with plants, and plants need water to grow. How can food chains in areas that receive little rain work as well as those in habitats like rain forests, where there are many thousands of plant and animal species? Places where very little rain falls are called deserts. They can be either hot or cold.

Survival

In hot deserts, very little rain falls, and during the day, temperatures soar. The Sahara of North Africa is the largest hot desert in the world. Plants such as cacti, sage brush, and date palms can grow in these conditions. They are adapted to lose as little water as possible through their fleshy leaves and stems. They are eaten by herbivores such as insects and small mammals, like the kangaroo rat and ground squirrel, as well as camels. Camels have large, leathery mouths that allow them to eat even the thorniest plants.

Plants in the desert grow low to the ground and are able to store water.

Top of the Chain

The secondary consumers in hot deserts are carnivores such as rattlesnakes and sidewinder snakes, and powerful insects such as scorpions that kill their prey using venom. The apex predators in the desert are the birds of prey, such as hawks and eagles, and the desert fox. They eat the lizards, snakes, and rats, but nothing preys on them. When they die, however, the decomposers, such as desert mushrooms, break down their bodies and return the nutrients they contain to the ground.

Desert mushrooms are decomposers.

cactus → kangaroo rat → rattlesnake → hawk → mushroom

MATH ATTACK!

The hottest temperature ever recorded in the Sahara was 136° Fahrenheit (58° C). At night, the temperature can fall to freezing point, or 32° Fahrenheit (0° C) because there are no clouds to hold in the heat. What is the difference between these two temperatures? Use this calculation to help you solve the problem:

136° FAHRENHEIT – 32° FAHRENHEIT = ?° FAHRENHEIT

Food Chains Under Threat

Food chains exist in a delicate balance. Any change that happens to one species affects all the others. Changes to an environment can affect the species living there. If the climate or landscape is altered, it may not be able to support the plants and animals living there. We are seeing changes like these threatening important food chains.

Changes in the Antarctic

Sea snails live in the ocean surrounding the Antarctic. They are eaten by fish, and those fish are eaten by seabirds. The apex predators in this food chain are whales. These are not the baleen whales that eat krill, but toothed whales that eat bigger animals, such as fish and seabirds. However, **global warming** is changing the quality of the water of the ocean. One effect of this is that the water is corroding, or eating away at, the shells of the sea snails. With fewer snails to eat, every animal up the food chain will suffer.

The killer whale, or orca, is a top predator in the Antarctic.

When we pollute our rivers and oceans with chemicals and trash, we impact all the species in the food chain there.

Problems in the Ocean

There are other problems in watery places, too. When we take too many fish out of the ocean, or even a river, to feed ourselves, the number of fish falls to a level that cannot recover. Unless we control our fishing, some species will die out. That will affect the other species that rely on those fish for their food. We also pollute our rivers and oceans with chemicals and trash that kill fish and other species. We need to take better care of these fragile habitats.

MORE THAN A NUMBER!

GLOBAL WARMING IS CAUSING THE OCEAN AROUND ANTARCTICA TO GET WARMER. THIS HAS REDUCED THE NUMBER OF PLANT PLANKTON THERE BY AT LEAST 10 PERCENT OVER THE PAST 30 YEARS. PLANT PLANKTON FEED KRILL, WHICH FEED BALEEN WHALES AND OTHER ANIMALS, SO MANY FOOD CHAINS WILL SUFFER.

A CONNECTED WORLD

Plants and animals all over the world live in an intricate network of food chains and food webs. Some live in places where conditions are difficult, others in places where the climate and the landscape can support a seemingly endless variety of species.

From one end of a food chain to the other, the living things exist in a delicate balance.

Needing Each Other

Wherever plants and animals live, they need each other. Many flowers need bees to carry their pollen, and bees need the flowers' nectar. Antelope eat grass, and lions eat antelope. Even lions need plants as much as bees and antelope do, because they are the start of every food chain. When all the food chains of a habitat are combined into a food web, we can see the delicate balance in which everything lives.

plant

antelope

lion

Learning for Life

It is important for us to understand how food chains and food webs work. This is not just because it is interesting to know how the energy in food is transferred from one species to another, or because it helps to show us how to find food for ourselves. It is also because, by understanding how living things relate to each other, we can learn how to protect and care for them. We can learn to avoid damaging them by the way we live in our complex, modern world. With this knowledge, we can make sure they can continue to live successfully.

MATH ATTACK!

Imagine that during a single day, 3 antelope eat 100 plants each, and 3 lions eat 1 antelope each. How many living things have either eaten or been eaten by the end of the day? Use this calculation to help you solve the problem:

Fungi are decomposers in a food chain. They feed the soil so plants can grow and the cycle can begin again.

3 ANTELOPE X 100 PLANTS = ? PLANTS
3 ANTELOPE + ? PLANTS + 3 LIONS + 3 ANTELOPE = ? LIVING THINGS

ANSWERS

Now that you have read about food chains, try to learn more. Draw the chains of some of the living things near you, and connect them into a food web. Here are the answers to the Math Attack problems. How did you score?

PAGE 7:

7 DAYS X 2 WEEKS = 14 DAYS

40 POUNDS X 14 DAYS = 560 POUNDS OF BAMBOO

PAGE 11:

105 POUNDS X 3 = 315 POUNDS

PAGE 15:

240 MILES PER HOUR – 190 MILES PER HOUR = 50 MILES PER HOUR FASTER

PAGE 19:

15 YEARS ÷ 5 YEARS = 3 TIMES LONGER

PAGE 23:

136° FAHRENHEIT – 32° FAHRENHEIT = 104° FAHRENHEIT

PAGE 27:

3 ANTELOPE X 100 PLANTS = 300 PLANTS

3 ANTELOPE + 300 PLANTS + 3 LIONS + 3 ANTELOPE = 309 LIVING THINGS

GLOSSARY

adapt To change something such as a body part or a behavior to survive.

aggressive Ready or likely to attack.

bacteria Very small organisms.

birds of prey Birds that hunt other animals for food.

decomposers The living things in a food chain that break down dead matter.

food web A system of linked food chains.

fungi Organisms that do not photosynthesize and include molds, rusts, mildews, smuts, mushrooms, and yeasts.

global warming Changes in the world's weather patterns caused by human activity.

habitat A place where an animal or plant lives.

mammals Animals that give birth to live young and feed them with milk.

nutrients Substances that provide food energy.

photosynthesis The process that plants use to make their food from the energy in sunlight.

predators Animals that hunt other animals for food.

prey An animal that is killed or eaten by another animal.

primary consumers Animals in a food chain that eat plants.

scavengers Animals that eat dead animals.

secondary consumers Animals in a food chain that eat primary consumers.

species A kind of living thing.

stealth A secret, smart, and quiet way of moving.

FURTHER READING

Books

Pettiford, Rebecca. *Desert Food Chains* (Pogo: Who Eats What?). Mankato, MN: Jump!, 2016.

Slade, Suzanne. *What Eats What in an Ocean Food Chain?* (Food Chains). Bloomington, IN: Picture Window Books, 2012.

Tarbox, A. *An Arctic Tundra Food Chain* (Odysseys in Nature). Mankato, MN: Creative Paperbacks, 2016.

Tarbox, A. *A Prairie Food Chain* (Odysseys in Nature). Mankato, MN: Creative Paperbacks, 2016.

Websites

Due to the changing nature of Internet links, PowerKids Press has developed an online list of websites related to the subject of this book. This site is updated regularly. Please use this link to access the list: **www.powerkidslinks.com/ma/food**

INDEX